This book flew into the hands of...

....

A Pardalote Press publication, 2022

ISBN 9780645563405

Text copyright© Sophie Masson

Illustrations copyright© Lorena Carrington

The moral rights of the author and illustrator
have been asserted.

www.pardalotepress.com

Printed in Australia by SOS Print+Media, Sydney

A catalogue record for this
book is available from the
National Library of Australia

BIRD'S EYE VIEW

POETRY AND PROSE FROM **SOPHIE MASSON**
ILLUSTRATIONS BY **LORENA CARRINGTON**

Contents

Pardalote

Diamond birds, they call us
For our jewelled velvet caps.
Yes, we're the smartest of birds
In our trim co-ordination:
Yellow, brown, black and grey
And white diamond decoration.
We're the hunting dandies
The chic insect slayers
In the tops of tall trees.
You might not see us
But you'll certainly hear us
Trill and whistle
Whistle and trill.
We nest underground
We dance on the wing,
We bring joy to all who see us.
No wonder they call us
A gem of a bird
A small, sweet, surprising thing!

Seagull beach party

Dressed in their smartest white and grey,
The seagulls are having a party today.
There's trim little Lightfoot, and beady-eyed Stumpy,
Lazy old Beaky, and squawky-voiced Grumpy,
Red Foot, and White Cap, and
Blackfeather Wing,
Watching to see what the humans will bring.

For seagulls love parties but never cook, ever,
Not starters or mains or dessert, or whatever!
They know it will come when the humans are here
The menu will vary, of course, but no fear,
There will be lots to grip, gobble and take,
Bread bits and chips, and, who knows, even cake!
And what they must do is to keep wide awake
And never but never give another a break.
The fastest will win, but also the meanest,
A seagull party is never the cleanest!

Big Sky Country—New England, NSW

The sky takes up most of the space here. Walking along the road between the houses, I am dizzy with the sensation of looking up: funnelled like a time-traveller into an exhilarating blue vastness. It is a swaggering thing, our sky; not pretty backdrop, not meek scenery, but overbearing, wild, almost scary. Skyscape is the main game; wildlife rituals and dramas more obviously enacted than on the secretive, low-rolling, subtly-shaded landscape.

It is as if the denizens of Sky have permission to defy the colour and noise taboos of the modest, almost morbidly modest, Australian bush. Writers of the bush have often been accused of a dun-coloured realism; perhaps few of them lifted their eyes from the land and into the gaudy wildness above them. Here are birds in improbable, fairytale colours: screeching galahs in preppy pink and grey; rosellas in an icecream cornucopia of raspberry, lime, lemon, and a wild, chemical blue; riots of black cockatoos, with strident yellow or red tail-feathers; fairy wrens with blue breasts, firetails carrying their sparking brand behind them; blush-cheeked king parrots, their backs a powdered-soft yet luminescent green. The eye is staggered by the range of it, the boldness of it, the proclamation of Nature's passionate excess.

There are other birds, more suitably attired, yet even these are surprising: the harridan-eyed magpie or currawong, in their sober black and white, meat-eater's sharp beaks open to carol some of the most beautiful of all bird songs to be heard anywhere; pretty, toy-like crested pigeons in dusty blues, pinks and greys, taking off in a clockwork whir and whistle of wings; swallows darting in soft late autumn air, giving you a deja vu of spring; the solemn flock of ibis, strutting in the paddock like an Egyptian mural come to life; the kookaburra, with its brisk kingfisher's manner, sitting on the telephone wire in summer, with the brown snake it's just killed dangling off the wire next to it, like a discarded, wrinkled tie.

Sometimes, a group of clouds hangs in the sky against other clouds, like a scrim on a stage, and then you might see a pair of wedge-tailed eagles, who make their home in the painted mountain just to the west of us, soaring in between the layers of clouds, like gods appearing in a Greek play. In the bright blue of an autumn sky--so clear and clear, in this high tableland, that it rinses the eye--a hazelnut-and-cream-coloured kestrel, which has been hanging steady as a melody for several seconds, plunges suddenly, sickeningly, down to the bleached-blond grass. Meanwhile, a willy wagtail alights on the roof of the greenhouse, waggling smugly to itself, dancing through sheer joie de vivre, it seems, whilst a string of silvery notes glitters from its throat.

Crows, as Norn-like and gloomily eager for slaughter as their brethren the world over, call querulously expectant portents of doom across a sky filling with battleship-grey cloud, while single-minded wild ducks descend in a flurry of neat legs and sleek dark heads, aiming for that patch of luminously green clover that seems so pleasantly to appear for them each year. A white-faced heron rises from the dam, turning imperceptibly from lanky fisherman to graceful skysailor in seconds. And in summer noisy mynahs, opportunistic and wary as sneak-thieves, beat a hasty retreat from the raspberries as we approach. They flap up into the lower reaches of the sky, with the lack of urgency born of dimwitted stubbornness and cunning. They knows as we do, that it'll be back later; we can't keep watch over the fruit all day, and even with the nets covering it, they will find a way...

At night, the drama in Sky Country becomes more one with the land, the edges blurring and smudging, though Sky itself, on clear nights, is black silk pinned and needled with thousands and thousands of stars. Bird-life becomes quieter, more modest: the hunters of the night are by their nature and necessities less like liveried warriors swaggering in the open, and more like hidden snipers. Once, though, we saw a tawny frogmouth, its face not all eyes, like an owl's, but all mouth, opening and shutting like a fairground toy's, and its body like weathered wood. And on fullmoon nights, when restless light bleaches land and sky alike, there can be strange otherworldly sights, strange sounds: an errant magpie in otherworldly gleam, singing a song seemingly composed for the moon, hollowing out the silent blackness of the night, and making us wake often in a light, uneasy sleep.

Owl, hunting

Deep in the woods an owl is calling,
Question on question into the dark:
Whoo is listening?
Whoo is about?
Whoo will it be
Tonight...tonight?

On wings of silence the owl is searching,
Gliding through the heart of the dark:
Searching for a rustle
A whisper
A scurry
A scratch of tiny claws
The faintest thud of
A tiny heart beating so fast…

Oh little animals of the forest
Creatures of fur, feathers and fear—
Keep out of sight
Keep very quiet
As the patient hunter of the night
Sweeps in softly from the dark.

A Feather of Fenist the Falcon

'Paris,' says my father. 'I am flying to Paris tonight, and I want to bring back something for each of you. Whatever you want, you shall have, my daughters.'

It is not an idle boast. My father is a man for whom everything is possible. A man of such wealth that nobody can say where his fortune begins and ends. A man of such influence that even our faraway Tsar of the icy eyes almost melts in his presence. A man who believes that everything is for sale and, if it is not, then it will be once the recalcitrant finds out just how much my father can offer. A man who loves his three motherless daughters in his own way but who acts as though each absence from us is his first, and not the consistent pattern of our lives. Each absence has meant an extravagant gift for each of us on his return, from the exquisite dolls of our childhood to the haute couture hauls of today.

'I want a ruby and pearl watch by Cartier and gold Louboutin heels,' says Olga, my eldest sister. 'And they must be unique, for I want no-one in the world to have the same as me.'

'Very well, my daughter, you shall have them,' says my father. 'And you, Irina?' he asks, turning to my middle sister.

'I want a one-of-a-kind Chanel crocodile-skin bag with a clasp made of three kinds of gold and three kinds of diamond, and a perfume by Dior created just for me, made of the rarest ingredients in the world and presented in a perfect crystal bottle.'

She says it triumphantly, with a sideways look at Olga, who raises a contemptuous eyebrow. Irina always likes to upstage our eldest sister. And Olga always likes to patronise her.

'Very well, my daughter, you shall have them,' says my father. He never seems ruffled or shocked or even uncertain about our demands, no matter how great, costly or fussy. 'And you, Katya?' he adds, turning to me.

I look him straight in the eye and say, 'I want a feather of Fenist the Falcon.'

'A feather of Fenist the Falcon?' he repeats. For the first time since I can remember, I have surprised my father.

'Trust you to ask for something ridiculous,' snaps Olga, 'something that doesn't exist.' And 'just like you to try and make yourself interesting,' sneers Irina, 'asking for something out of a dusty old fairy tale.'

I just look at them and say, quietly, 'Words make impossible things exist and fairy tales are still alive.'

'Listen to you! You are like an old woman in a young body,' scoffs Olga, while Irina mocks, 'Or a child, for even in the way you speak, it's like you're living in some old-fashioned children's book.'

They are about to say more, but Father stops them, sternly. 'I will not have this, my daughters. Katya has the right to ask for what she wants. As do you.'

Olga and Irina go quiet. They know that particular tone of voice from Papa, and they want their gifts, of course. But it's more than that. Even if they think what I have asked for is ridiculous, impossible, nonexistent, they are miffed that I have thought of a gift far more unique than any of theirs, for it has disconcerted our normally imperturbable father. It is a dilemma, and I see them struggling with it.

My father, too, is struggling. But for a different reason. Whatever you want, he told us. Everything is possible, that has been the motto of his life. He came up from nowhere to be everywhere and so he believes it is true. Orphaned in babyhood, brought up by his grandmother in a remote village of our ancestral country of snow and blood and iron, marked on his very skin by the ink of prison brotherhood as a young man, he rose to become a gold-pocketed angel of the upside-down revolution. An oligarch, they called him. Even now that, his wings slightly clipped, he lives more privately in this cheerful country of endless sun and sparkling calm, he still commands an audience in the courts of power. Why should the impossible not be obtainable with a snap of his fingers?

But though he knows what the feather of Fenist is, he has no idea how on earth he can obtain this impossible thing that I have asked for. He does not know it is a test. I would like him to admit for once that there is something he cannot buy. I want him to know I love him no matter what, and for that I do not need him to unhook the moon from the sky, or find a talisman that is just a whisper of memory in my dead mother's voice, recounting a beautiful fairy tale from deepest childhood.

He looks at me. Hesitates. Then he says, 'If a feather from Fenist the Falcon is what you want, my daughter, then a feather from Fenist the Falcon is what you shall have.' And I know then that I failed and he will not admit that he is not invincible. For unlike the gifts my sisters asked for, this will really tax my father's ingenuity, and that is what I know, too late, he wants most of all. I want to take my request back, to explain it was just a joke, but already he is waving goodbye, and striding across the tarmac to where his private jet awaits.

He is gone seven days and seven nights. During that time, my sisters work out to their own satisfaction that their dreamy little sibling with her nose always in a book has not got one over them, as they'd feared, but from sheer nerdish perversity has thrown away her chance to get something valuable. 'Serve you right,' they say, 'if Papa comes back with the feather of some mouldy stuffed bird of prey!' For on the Internet they had come across the site of a famous taxidermy shop in Paris called Deyrolle, and become convinced that was where our father would go. As for me, I spend the week ignoring their remarks and re-reading the tattered book at the bottom of my drawer, the one that belonged to Mama. The story of Fenist the Falcon is the one I always return to, the one I loved most as a child. It is the story of three motherless girls, their doting father, and the magic feather, which summons a shape-shifting lover and brings adventure and danger into the youngest girl's life. 'Words make impossible things exist,' I say to myself, 'and fairy tales are always alive.' I had said it defiantly to my sisters, but did I really believe it? Not really that week, at least.

We are sitting by the pool in the sharp golden twilight of an Antipodean late summer the afternoon my father returns from Paris. He comes to us with a heavy step, an impression of exhaustion not improved by the dark circles under his eyes. But his smile is broad as he greets us, laden with the distinctive carry bags of the famous fashion houses. 'My darling girls, here is Paris for you, right in your arms!' And he hands the bags to my exclaiming sisters.

Then he turns to me. 'For you, my dearest Katya, it was not so simple,' he begins, and my sisters shoot me a triumphant glance. 'I tried everything. I asked everywhere. In desperation I even went to a shop called Deyrolle...' and here my sisters cannot contain their glee, '...and they had every kind of beast and bird and reptile you can imagine, stuffed and mounted and glaring from every corner--but even they did not have a feather of Fenist the falcon. I was afraid I would have to come back to you empty-handed.'

'It does not matter, Papa,' I say. 'It was just a story. Just words from a fairy tale.' My sisters don't understand why I sound so cheerful.

But my father is still talking. 'Then on the last afternoon, a meeting finished early, and it was such a fine day, despite the chill season, that I sent the car away and walked back to the hotel. On the way I came across a little park, sandwiched between two tall buildings. And there sat an elegant old lady, feeding birds from a bag full of crumbs. I don't know why, but she suddenly reminded me of my grandmother.' My sisters look at each other. I know what their eyes are saying, for the old woman we also called Babushka was the very opposite of a chic Parisian.

My father goes on. 'So I said Bonjour. The old lady's eyes looked straight through me and she said Bonjour back. I watched her feed the birds, and after a moment, I realised she was blind, and that was why she'd seemed to look straight through me. Then, I don't know why, but I asked her if she'd ever heard of the feather of Fenist the falcon, and she said to me, quite simply, Of course I have, monsieur. She reached into her coat pocket...' He reached into his own coat pocket, in deliberate imitation. 'And brought out her hand, closed over something.' Here he brought out a little box. 'And when she opened her hand, I saw...'

It wasn't just me, now, staring at him as he opened the little white box. My sisters were all eyes, too, and in their expressions I read an unexpected softness. Could it be that a homely magic had come into the house with his story, and touched us all with its kindness? I almost said, Don't open the box, Papa, it is better like that. Let our imagination hold it in our hearts.

But of course I didn't say it, and of course he opened the box. There, lying nestled in tissue paper, was a small feather. It didn't look magical. It didn't look otherworldly. It looked like an ordinary brown, downy feather. It was an ordinary brown, downy feather, probably a sparrow's.

My father did not appear to notice my crestfallen expression, or my sisters' sideway grins. 'And I said, "I have promised my youngest daughter a feather of Fenist the falcon, so will you sell it to me? I can pay you a great deal of money." "No," she said, "no it is not for sale." "But you don't understand," I said, "I will pay anything, any sum. I am a man so rich I could pave the whole of Paris with gold and still have enough to live like a king for a century." She repeated, "No, it is not for sale." "It must be," I said, "it must, or I will disappoint my youngest daughter, my Katya, and that I cannot bear".'

There is a lump in my throat as he continues, '"It is not for sale," she told me a third time, "but I will give it to you." And as I sat there speechless she handed me the feather and looked at me with those eyes that go straight through you. She said, "It is the heart-feather. Do you see?" I did not see, but I said I did, and thanked her, or tried to. She did not listen, wiping the crumbs from her skirt and getting to her feet. I wanted to ask her questions, but before I could gather my senses, she was gone.' A pause. 'And so here I am, and here it is, Katya, my dearest child—a feather of Fenist the falcon, just as you asked.'

'Oh Papa!' I said, and hugged him. What did it matter if the feather was just an ordinary sparrow's? What did it matter if the old lady was not really a good fairy, but a kind stranger who had seen into a tired father's heart, beyond his rich clothes and hard face? It was coincidence she had the feather in her pocket. Not even a strange coincidence, for what was more natural for a bird-lady than to have a stray feather in her pocket? She had given him what he wanted, belief that he could bring me what I wanted. And in so doing she had made me see that belief was precious to him and that was his real gift to us, every time. His gift of love. It makes me happy. Yet sad, at the same time. I don't know why.

I go up to bed that night with a feeling that nothing will ever be the same again. The old lady's mysterious last words, 'It is the heart-feather,' haunt me like distant music, like the first whisper of a spell. I place the feather carefully in its box on my windowsill, along with the other small treasures I have gathered over the years, things that were never for sale and are therefore priceless: a shell necklace my mother made me when I was tiny, a perfect round white pebble Olga had given me for my tenth birthday, a leaf skeleton as delicate as lace I'd picked up on a walk with my father, a tiny silver key which Irina unexpectedly gave me on my eighteenth birthday a month ago. 'It's the key to being grown up,' she'd said. I look at the feather, touch it gently. 'Fenist the falcon, beautiful stranger from another world,' I whisper. 'Words make impossible things exist, and fairy tales are truly alive.' It seems to me that the feather flutters under my fingers, but likely that is imagination, or a stray breath of night air creeping in from the window. I stand there in silence for a moment. And then I go to bed.

I fall asleep almost immediately. When I wake it is from a dream, in the middle of the night. In my dream, there was a sound. A sharp tapping and scraping, sinister and insistent. I sit up. There it comes again! The tapping. And this time it is no dream.

When I turn on the light, my room springs into familiar view around me. But still the tapping persists. It is coming from the window. Something is out there, tapping on the glass. A twig, I tell myself. A branch, from the tree outside. Something ordinary.

But I get up anyway and go to the window. I draw aside the curtains. And there, on the outside window sill, tapping at the glass, staring at me from bright, cold black eyes, is a bird. A bird of prey, with a sharp curved beak, plumage of black and brown, mottled white and soft downy brown feathers at its breast. I glance at the feather my father gave me. It gleams with a strange sheen, caught in a ray of moonlight. I think of the girl in the fairy tale, opening the window. My spine tingles. My scalp prickles. I know I could still walk away. Close the curtains. Go back to bed. And everything would be as before. Tomorrow, I would wake, and tell myself it had all been a dream. In time I would forget it, forget that my words had once had such power.

 I open the window. The bird hops in. Onto the inner windowsill first, and then onto the floor. And as it touches the floor, something happens. I cannot describe it. It is like something out of a dream, and in dreams things just happen. Abysses open where there was flat sunny land,

seas suddenly flood up a cliff, tigers prowl at bathroom doors, people appear from nowhere, not in a puff of smoke or a burst of light, they just do. This is like that. One moment, the bird is on the floor. The next, he is there.

I stare at him. He stares at me. In that first instant neither of us can say anything. I have never seen a man naked before, not in the flesh, because I have not yet had a boyfriend. Of course, in our time even someone much younger than me can know exactly what a naked man looks like. But I have never seen anyone like him, not in any of the fantasy images my sisters and I have giggled over. He is not tall, but well-made, his eyes are pitch black, with lashes and brows of the same colour, his hair a soft wavy dark brown, his skin the colour of dark honey. Instinctively, his hands are covering his private parts. There is curly short hair the colour of his eyebrows escaping from under the long fingers with their ragged nails. His legs, too, sport dark hair, and his toenails, like those on his fingers, are ragged and sharp, almost like claws. There is something wild, even dangerous, about him, despite his striking looks, or perhaps because of them.

Like a rapid-fire camera, I take it all in, the look

of him, the presence, the wild feral scent, there is such fire in my blood, such ice in my bones that I cannot move. Then I give a little cry, and fall back; and he gives a deeper cry, and falls back. I come to my senses first and throw a blanket at him. He wraps it around himself, huddling at the far end of the room as though he is afraid.

'Who are you?' I ask, in my own mother-tongue, but he does not seem to understand, though his eyes go to my face, so I know he has heard me.

It is pointless to ask, because I know who he is. I asked for the feather of Fenist the Falcon, a name I'd heard only in a fairy tale. I believed words made the impossible exist, and here is the breathing proof, bursting into my life, tearing aside the veil of the everyday.

It is not just in the old days that strange things happened. Our ancestral land is a land of deep magic, deep as the deepest mine. It has always been so; it is still so. In our time, fortunes come from nowhere and to nowhere return; swan-necked girls in glass heels ornament the arms of chunky robber barons and witches peddle spells under neon signs, madmen turn trains and buses into fireworks of blood and the puny grandson of a cook has become a mighty Tsar. In our blood-country, there is no separation between then and now, the future might be hazy but the past is vivid and walks among us. We have brought these things in our monogrammed baggage, in our passionate hearts, to this new country of ours, which is full of its own subtle enchantment: the magic of a dreaming land as old as time and swans the colour of night, of diamond leaves and sharp bright shadows of the past, and people with tongues so various that it is as if the globe has been distilled here. Yes, our world is a wonder, so why shouldn't a bird turn into a man just as in the old stories? Why shouldn't a terrified young shapeshifter crouch in the bedroom of a girl who knows herself to be grown into a woman this very night?

But it is all very well to think it. It is quite another to know what to do. I am about to reach for my phone and try and summon up something on the Internet which might give me some clue as to what you should do if a shapeshifter suddenly erupts into your world—and believe me, there are sites explaining just such things—when he speaks in French. 'Pardonnez-moi, mademoiselle.' His voice is deep and rather hoarse on the faint rasp of an accent with the colour of desert kingdoms, and it sends a little tremor up my spine.

'You are French,' I say, in that tongue. He nods, his Adam's apple bobbing up and down in his throat. It touches me, this sign of uncertainty. That, and what he has said, asking me to forgive him.

'It is not a problem.'

His eyes widen, and I want to kick myself. Of all the silly, clumsy things to say! How can this situation not be a problem? For him, and for me. What will my family say when they find him here? How can I possibly explain his alien presence? And how can he find his way home, now a mischievous magic has fastened his fate to mine with that feather?

'Excuse me,' I begin, flushing, but he interrupts. 'I am a bird in the day, and a man at night.' A pause, then he continues, sadly. 'It is my fate to be a being of two kinds. But I do not understand why I am here...'

I show him the feather. 'It's my fault,' I say in English, for I am so troubled I cannot summon up any more French.

He looks at me. He says, in a slightly awkward, softly accented English, 'You find this?'

I shake my head. 'Someone gave it to my father, in Paris.'

'But why?'

'I asked him to bring back a feather of Fenist the falcon.' I hesitate. 'I thought it—it didn't exist. I thought—it was really just a name from a fairy tale my mother once told me.'

'Ah,' he says, and in his black eyes I read the same feelings that must be in my own grey ones. Confusion. A little fear. And something else. Something that we cannot put a name to, not yet. Then he says, 'So it is your words that summon me. It is your words that have brought me here. To you. And now--what are we going to do?' We. That little pronoun ripples under my skin.

'One thing I do know,' I say, 'is that we cannot tell anyone, not anyone, what has happened. Because if they find out who you are—if they learn you are a real shape-shifter, then—'

'Then we will be in the cold eye of the public,' he finishes, quietly, 'and we will not have freedom to be our secret selves.'

'Oh yes,' I breathe, 'yes, exactly,' and our eyes meet.

We were strangers to each other, in the very strangest of once upon a time. And yet now it is as though we truly know each other, in the depths of soul and heart and body, and the shock of it has transformed everything.

I am no longer a dreaming girl; I am a woman. He is no longer a name in a fairy-tale dream; he is a man such as I had never imagined. He is there, the one I did not even know I wanted until I summoned him with my own shape-shifting words.

With him I will live an adventure like no other, in this passionate, secret, dangerous world we will make. For whatever dark chapters our story is to have, whatever things we have to endure—and I know already there will be much to endure, for the world will find out one day and will not leave us alone—there will always be this darkly shining memory, this first encounter.

He smiles, his eyes lighting up as I leave my corner and go towards him, so that we can taste each other for the very first time.

Thief

Hey, you in the smart morning suit!
Hey, you with the bright morning voice!
Hey you,
Pretending to stroll,
Casual and easy,
With your rascal friends watching
Pretending you haven't noticed
The sweet golden fruit on the vine--
Yes, you! I'm talking to you--
And I've told you before—
Those grapes aren't for you, Mr Currawong—
So shoo!

Bird Calls

Cockatoo
Hey, hey, did you spot
That field of fresh corn?
Quick, mates, quick,
Before it's all gorn!

Magpie
I spy a human
I spy a threat
Divebomb the human
Too close to my nest!

Ibis
In the country I'm a fine lady
In the city I slink and stink.
In the paddocks I hunt in the grass
In the streets I hunt in the bins.

BOTTLES

Currawong
Sing a song of silver
Up into the sky,
Then no-one will notice
That you've thieved the pie!

Koel
On and on and on and on
I make my feelings clear
Yet nobody wants to listen
No-one wants me near.

Bronzewing pigeon
Boom boom boom boom
Foghorn bird, that's me,
Sending out my messages
Hidden in the tree.

Kestrel

Sail in the sky
Hang in the air
Dive down so sudden
I'm almost not there...

Kookaburra

Look at us here
Fluffed-up in a row
Laughing and chuckling
It was such a good joke!

Wings

Flap slow flap slow
Hey lazy day dally of crow.
Quick flash, flash, flit,
Snacks on the go, here comes a swift!
Feather flock cockatoo clan
Rushing the sky with noisy plan.
High above, eagle soaring,
Hanging, gliding,
Jet-fighter diving.
Crimson rosella's elegant crew
Sailing the wind with banners of blue.
Tuning notes through eddies of air,
Silver-songed magpie
Chased for a dare.
Darting bright flicker of Christmas-tree glitter,
Clockwork wings of honeyeater.

Skyflix

See the offerings on Skyflix,
A packed program of genres:
Daily showings of sunrise, sunset
Blue and gold days
Black velvet nights pinned and needled with stars.
Extravagant dramas
Of quarrelsome bird kingdoms
Games of feathered thrones
In swaggering jewelled dress.

Musical productions
With beaked lounge-suit entertainers
In glorious voice
And predatory glare.

Romantic comedies
Of pigeon fan dances
And fairy wren suitors
Challenging their own reflections.
Battlefield dramas
Starring magpie snipers
Darting in ambush
Patrolling eagles
Chased by mynah squadrons
Guerrilla bands of galahs
Descending on the ripened corn.
And late at night, the midnight movie with its
haunting soundtrack:
Boobook boobook boobook.

Lyrebird Sunset

Down in the sunset under the trees
The lyrebird spreads his tail to tease.
They call him the lyrebird
Because he can sing to you.
They call him the liar-bird
Because he plays tricks on you!

Listen!
Now he's a engine,
Now he's a dove,
A cuckoo that calls,
And waterfalls.

Lyrebird, lyrebird, what is your own song?
Sing to me lyrebird, all night long!

Acknowledgements

The following pieces were first published in magazines and journals:

A Feather of Fenist the Falcon, in TEXT, Vol. 21, Issue Special 43, 2017

'Big Sky Country, New England,' in Dark Sky Dreamings: An Inland Skywriters Anthology, Interactive Publishers, 2019

Wings in The School Magazine, May 2014

Thief in The School Magazine, March 2017

Owl, hunting in The School Magazine, August 2020

'Lyrebird Sunset' in Our Home Is Dirt by Sea, edited by Dianne Bates, Walker Books 2016

'Seagull Beach Party' in One Minute Till Bedtime, edited by Kenn Nesbitt, Little, Brown (USA) 2016

Thanks

We owe many thanks to all the wonderful people who supported us in so many ways: through our crowdfunding campaign, by offering us advertising spots and interviews, by sharing our exploits on social media, and in the provision of hot tea and toast.

We couldn't have done it without you. Thank you.